Passing the Bar Exam:
An Unconventional Approach

DESIREE A. NAVARRO
RN, BSN, Attorney At Law

Copyright © 2013 Desiree A. Navarro

All rights reserved.

ISBN-13: 978-1514396230

ISBN-10: 1514396238

For Al, without your unending love, support and especially patience, I'm sure none of this would have been possible.

Table of Contents

Preface 1

Chapter I - The California Bar Exam – A Brief Overview 7

Chapter II - December 13

Chapter III - January 36

      Practice, Practice, Practice 42

Chapter IV - February 47

Chapter V – Bar Exam Week 54

      Study Materials 57

      Food 58

      Earplugs 60

      Monday Night – Checking In 60

Chapter VI – Tuesday – Day 1 64

Chapter VII – Wednesday – Day 2 MBE Day 78

Chapter VIII – Thursday – Day 3 95

Chapter IX March, April, May – The Wait / The Results 112

Chapter X – Getting Sworn In 119

Final Suggestions / Parting Thoughts 121

Preface

This story came about one year after passing the California Bar Exam on my first attempt without a formal bar review course. I figured that a year after taking the exam, the entire consuming experience would gradually fade away from the confines of my mind, and that I'd move on with my life. Instead, it became an unforgettable event, one that I lived over and over again. I replayed the exam preparations and experience, repeatedly in my mind. Questions about the entire process continuously poured in; not only by those getting ready to take the exam, but also by those who were just plain curious about the exam preparations and exam process. Consequently, I found myself telling my story over and over again.

Passing the California Bar Exam, was one of the most difficult experiences of my life. It took all I had, "and then some". But the reward of seeing my name on the pass list and ultimately being sworn in as an attorney and "officer of the court", made it worth all of the time, effort and expense. It was truly an unforgettable experience.

While I certainly cannot guarantee that the method(s) I used to pass the bar exam will yield similar results for you, I can say without reservation, if you at least take what I did and adapt my method of preparing to your learning style, you will considerably increase your chances of passing this exam, and after all, that is what matters, passing!!! You do not have to "ace" this exam, rather, you just need to do well enough to make the pass list.

My story is organized around the two and one half months prior to the bar exam, beginning with the decision as to whether or not to even take the exam, followed by the actual bar exam experience, and culminating with receiving results. I think this structure is the most helpful in preparing for the bar exam, regardless of what law school you attended, or how well you did while there. I have also made an effort to keep this story short, direct, and to the point, as I know that if you are preparing for the bar exam you have plenty to read. You should be able to get through this story quickly, take what is helpful, and then turn your attention right to bar exam preparation.

A word about where you earned your Juris Doctorate degree in relation to passing this exam. The pass rate on the California Bar Exam is highest for those attending an American Bar Association (ABA) accredited law school, and second highest for those attending a California accredited law school. However, even if you didn't attend an ABA or California accredited law school, don't be discouraged. I am living proof that passing the bar exam is more about how hard you are willing to work, and how well you read and write (and perhaps doing all of these things for three consecutive days), than it is about where you attended law school. I obtained my law degree via an online program, classified as a "correspondence school", and considered the least prestigious way of earning a Juris Doctorate degree. Nonetheless, I took and passed, on my first attempt, without a formal bar review course, the same bar exam as the top student from a top notch school. So, to repeat, passing the bar exam is less about where you went to school, and **all about** how hard you are willing to work, and how well you read and write.

I started law school at the age of forty-five, and was sworn in as an attorney one week before my fiftieth birthday. I have been a nurse since I was 24, so embarking on the study of law was a monumental undertaking. I also lost my mom to stage IV lung cancer in the middle of my third year. It was a definite low point. I wanted to take a leave of absence from law school to help care for my mom, but in order to do so, I had to have 50% of third year course work completed. My mom died the same day I "made it" to the 50% mark, so I decided to forgo the leave of absence and complete the year. Having law school to focus on operated as an excellent diversion. Looking back, I could have used some time for the grieving process.

Fast forward to two weeks before the bar exam. I went for my annual mammogram in which the results came back abnormal, requiring a procedure known as a stereotactic breast biopsy. Unfortunately, the soonest that this could be scheduled was the Monday following the bar exam. After I somewhat fell apart, my husband Al, gave me some great advice, he told me to "think like a man", that is, to emotionally and intellectually compartmentalize the abnormal mammogram results and upcoming breast biopsy, and instead stay focused on bar exam preparation. The biopsy results came back "inconclusive", requiring a second more extensive biopsy, known as a needle localization excisional biopsy, which showed "atypical" cells but no cancer cells. While I was elated to pass the bar exam, I was overwhelmingly relieved to receive favorable breast biopsy results. I felt blessed then as I do now.

Finally, I want to extend my sincere congratulations to each and every one of you for surviving law school (wherever you attended), and having the courage to sit for the California Bar Exam – considered to be one of the toughest bar exams in the country. I always thought it was a dirty trick that one works their tails off in law school, and THEN has to face the bar exam. It's like running the gauntlet, and then getting to walk over glowing coals – barefoot!!! So please accept my sincere congratulations on not only graduating from law school, but also on having the courage and tenacity to sit for the California Bar Exam.

Chapter I - The California Bar Exam – A Brief Overview

Here is a brief overview of the California Bar Exam. While I provide this overview, make sure to take the time to visit the "CalBar" website, as it is a wealth of valuable information. For example, the website provides specific and detailed information regarding the subjects of Contracts, Civil Procedure, Evidence, Professional Responsibility and Wills and Succession. Given the financial and emotional costs of taking the bar exam, time spent learning about and understanding the exam format is definitely time well spent.

The California Bar Exam is a strictly timed 18 hour exam, over a three day period offered twice a year in February and July. While the actual exam dates vary, the exam is always offered on a Tuesday, Wednesday and Thursday, six hours each day. Tuesday and Thursday are identical in format in that during the three hour morning sessions, you are expected to complete three essays within three hours. You will get a lunch break lasting approximately 90 minutes and then return in the afternoon to complete a three hour Performance Test.

The Performance Test is a method of testing how well the examinee can solve a complex legal problem. It consists of a "file" and a "library". Included in the file is the all-important "task memo". The file is typically 20-30 pages long and contains specific information regarding the client. The task memo (included in the file) is the assignment which you are expected to complete within the allotted three hours.

The library which is approximately 50-100 pages, contains the law needed to solve the legal problem as detailed in the task memo. Thus, the library contains relevant (and some not so relevant) cases, statutes, and legislative provisions.

The challenge with completing the Performance Test is reading through the file and library, and then allowing sufficient time to write a complete answer. The rule of thumb is that no more than 90 minutes should be spent reading the file and library and outlining the answer. The remaining 90 minutes should be used for writing a thorough answer which is responsive to the task memo. Please be certain that your answer is responsive to the task memo, and not rambling and or wandering off conceptually in a different direction. Keep your answer responsively focused on your assignment as detailed in the task memo.

Wednesday differs from Tuesday and Thursday in that it is designated as the multistate bar exam (MBE) day. Six subjects are tested via 200 multiple choice questions. During the morning session you are expected to complete 100 multiple choice questions in three hours. This requires you to work at a steady breakneck pace of one minute and 48 seconds per question. After lunch you will return for an afternoon session of another 100 questions, also to be completed within three hours.

When I took the bar exam in 2005, 13 subjects were tested. Remedies was not considered a subject unto itself, but rather, was tested by incorporation into other subjects, such as Torts, Contracts and/or Real Property. Below is a list of bar exam subjects. An asterisk after a subject indicates a MBE subject. All of the subjects are testable on the essay portion, while ONLY the subjects marked with an asterisk are tested on the MBE section. Note: the Committee of Bar Examiners combines the subjects of Criminal Law and Criminal Procedure on the MBE portion of the exam.

In July 2005 the Committee of Bar Examiners made a few changes to the bar exam. Corporations was changed to "Business Associations", and Wills and Trusts was changed to "Wills and Succession".

Additionally, beginning with the February 2015 bar exam administration, Civil Procedure will also be included on the MBE section of the bar exam. Furthermore, beginning with the July 2017 administration, the bar exam will be reduced from three days to two days. The two day format will consist of Day One being five one hour essays and one 90 minute Performance Test, while Day Two will continue to be designated as the MBE day. Again, a visit to the CalBar website will provide detailed information about exam content and format as well as previous bar exam essay questions along with selected passing answers. To repeat, I urge you to visit the CalBar website so that you are well acquainted with the exam content and format. Moreover, studying previous bar exam essay questions AND selected passing answers, gives you a genuine sense of what will be expected of you on the actual exam. Remember, the better prepared you are for this exam the more you increase your chances of making the pass list.

Bar Exam Subjects by Alphabetical Order

California Community Property

Civil Procedure (added to the MBE section starting with the February 2015 admin)

Constitutional Law*

Contracts*

Corporations (Business Associations)

Criminal Law*

Criminal Procedure*

Evidence*

Professional Responsibility

Real Property*

Remedies (not considered a subject unto itself)

Torts*

Trusts

Wills (Wills and Succession)

Understand, the bar exam is a <u>WRITING</u> exam, in that writing accounts for 65% of your total score (the two Performance Tests accounting for 26%, the remaining six essays accounting for 39%). In other words, 12 of the 18 hours of the bar exam is spent writing, while a mere six of the remaining 18 hours is spent answering multiple choice questions.

When you look at the percentage of points allocated to the writing portion of the exam, it should become clear to you how important it is to invest considerable time and energy in writing practice Performance Tests and essays. I cannot tell you how many people I know **did not** pass because they didn't understand this simple fact. For some reason they thought they could pass this exam by doing well on the MBE portion alone, which only accounts for 35% of your score. Accept the fact that this is a writing exam and allocate your time accordingly.

Chapter II - December

I was a reluctant examinee. I had heard so many harrowing stories about the bar exam that I had made up my mind to NOT sit for the February administration. I decided that finishing law school and earning my Juris Doctorate degree was enough of an accomplishment. Besides, I told myself, I really didn't want to actually **practice** law. All of this changed in December once I realized that the bar exam was the proverbial culminating experience of four years of law school; I admitted to myself that I actually wanted that consummating experience.

I also considered NOT taking the February exam and instead waiting for the next administration, which would have been in July. I rationalized that if I waited and took the July exam I'd have a full six months to prepare, rather than only two and one half months. Everyone I talked to discouraged this approach, reasoning that most people would not actually spend six months on bar exam preparation.

I admit, I probably would have been one of those people, **thinking** that I would study for six months. In reality, I would have taken a couple of months off to rest and recuperate from the grind of law school. Then I would have needed a few more weeks to get motivated to study. By the time I actually got around to studying, it would have been May, which would have given me two and one half months for bar exam preparation. I realized if I waited and took the exam in July, I would be no better off, and most likely worse off, because whatever momentum I had gained from law school would have been lost. I decided to move forward and take the February administration.

Now that I had committed to taking the February bar exam, the next big decisions were (1) which, if any, bar review course to take, (2) what type of work/study schedule to follow, (3) whether to handwrite, type, or use a laptop for the exam (4) where to stay during the exam.

1) Which, If Any Bar Review Course to Take?

I agonized over choosing a bar review course. Throughout law school I had accumulated mounds of study materials. I had everything from essay writing books, which included instructions on how to write law school essays, adhering to a strict "IRAC" style, (an acronym for issue, rule, analysis, conclusion), to fact patterns from previous bar exams.

My collection of study materials included, but was not limited to, audio tapes, flash cards, multiple choice questions, outlines, rule statements, charts and flowsheets. Flowsheets are particularly useful in a legal context as they provide a method of deliberate reasoning with regard to analyzing a set of facts. In addition to all of the above study aides, I also had the requisite hornbooks and casebooks from each class along with notes and outlines I had accumulated throughout my four years of law school. In fact, I had an entire bookcase of law school study materials.

Because I had such volumes of materials, and to be honest, I am also "thrifty", I did not see the point in spending thousands of dollars on a bar review course which undoubtedly consisted of yet **more** study materials.

According to one of my law school professors, the chances of passing the bar exam without a bar review course are less than 5%. Everyone said I **had** to take a bar review course — that passing the exam without one was next to impossible. I struggled with this decision. In my heart of hearts I knew what I needed — and it was not additional study materials. I was told that by taking a formal bar review course I wouldn't just get additional study materials, but rather, I'd get lectures by experts in each particular subject — experts who had extensively studied the bar exam. In other words, the knowledge which would be imparted on me would be far superior to anything I already had on hand.

Taking a formal bar review course would also allow me to submit practice essays for grading. But I felt had been graded enough throughout law school, and I didn't want to subject myself to more. I was told I was a fool, sure to fail if I didn't take a formal bar review course. This prediction annoyed me. I took it as a challenge. I wanted to see if I could pass the bar exam without a formal bar review course; I wanted to be as prepared as I could, yet, I didn't want to spend thousands of dollars on more study materials.

I decided to compromise and take a well-known six day MBE review course which finished three days before Christmas. It provided an excellent substantive review of the six MBE subjects, along with test taking strategies for each subject, followed by a detailed review of each assigned MBE question. Included in this review course was discussion explaining why a particular answer choice was correct, and **just as important**, why the other answer choices were incorrect.

I know I have mentioned this before, but it bears repeating: on the MBE portion of the exam you will have a mere one minute and 48 seconds to read a complex set of facts, select the correct answer out of four choices and move on to the next question. There is absolutely NO time to ponder, contemplate and/or second guess oneself. You have to understand the material, know what the bar examiners are asking, eliminate the incorrect answers and select the correct answer – all within one minute and 48 seconds. If you understand the material, you can usually identify two obvious incorrect answer choices. Selecting the correct answer choice is often more difficult, as the difference between a correct and incorrect answer is often subtle, sometimes coming down to **one word.**

In order to become proficient at selecting the correct answer under the pressure of limited time, you must commit to extensive practice of MBE questions. I knew I was committed to putting in the required practice, and felt the MBE review course would provide me an approach to tackling MBE questions. In retrospect, the investment in the MBE course was definitely money well spent.

But my dilemma regarding a bar review course was, however, still unresolved. I knew there were many excellent bar review courses on the market. But I honestly felt I would be wasting my money if I enrolled in a bar review course (and received all of the materials it came with) given all of the study materials I had already purchased during law school. I was convinced I knew what I needed – and it was not more study materials. I felt I needed a thorough substantive review of each subject, then time to practice applying the rules of law to as many fact patterns as I could bear.

I compromised again, and purchased off the internet, at a fraction of the cost, a used highly respected home study bar review course consisting of books only (no audio materials). If that wasn't enough, I purchased a second used bar review course, also books only, from an acquaintance who had recently passed the bar exam. Even though I didn't want to buy more study materials, I figured this was a good compromise, as I would get a chance to evaluate formal bar review materials without having to spend thousands of dollars.

I spent a few days reviewing all of the materials, wondering what was so indispensable about these bar review courses. I'll admit some of the essay and Performance Test materials were very good, but most of the material was similar to what I already had on hand. I decided I would design my own personalized, customized bar review course. More on this later.

2) What Type of Work/ Study Schedule to Follow?

I know of people who worked either full or part time during bar review and passed – this was not something I realistically considered. I recommend taking **at least** two months off from a job to study for the bar exam. For me, bar review WAS my job. I was fortunate in that I worked "on call" as a nurse and had (and have) a supportive husband who agreed to pick up the slack financially. I cleared my schedule so I had half of December and all of January and February to devote to bar review. Given the cost of taking the exam, three nights in a hotel, and time spent studying, I figured I'd give the exam 110% on my first attempt; this seemed the most economical approach, both financially and emotionally.

This brings me to the next part of bar review – my "personalized, customized" bar review course and study schedule. Again, the California Bar Exam tests 13 individual subjects in addition to Remedies. Because studying thirteen subjects overwhelmed me, I decided to divide the subjects into four individual groups. I **always** studied those particular subjects in a group together and as a unit. I psychologically told myself that each "group" of subjects was really only one subject.

I grouped subjects together which seemed most likely to be tested in a "crossover" question. A crossover question is a situation where two or more subjects are tested in one essay fact pattern. For example, often Criminal Law, Criminal Procedure and/or

Evidence are tested together, thus, this would be considered a "crossover" question. I also grouped subjects in an effort to simulate the actual practice of law, grouping subjects together that could arise in an actual case. Remedies was divided into Contract and Real Property Remedies. Professional Responsibility is included in Group 4, but because it is such an important subject, (not just for the bar exam, but also for the practice of law) be prepared to discuss Professional Responsibility along with any other subject. Here is a list of my groupings of bar exam subjects. Remember, there have been some changes to the bar exam, so be sure to visit the CalBar website to confirm the subjects being tested. Even though there may be some changes, you can still use these groupings of subjects as you prepare for the exam. An asterisk denotes a MBE subject, and remember Criminal Law and Criminal Procedure are combined on the MBE section of the exam.

GROUP 1

Contracts*

Real Property*

Contract Remedies

Real Property Remedies

GROUP 2

Torts*

Constitutional Law*

Civil Procedure*

Corporations (Business Assoc.)

GROUP 3

Criminal Law*

Criminal Procedure*

Evidence*

GROUP 4

California Community Property

Wills (Wills and Succession)

Trusts

Professional Responsibility

Now that I had the subjects grouped and a plan as to how I was going to tackle the material, all I needed was a study schedule. I immediately committed a schedule to writing as this made it much easier to follow, in that it was non-negotiable.

I had an established routine already in place, which I altered to accommodate the time I would need to study for the exam. I love to exercise; I swim, run and lift weights, so exercising every morning for one hour before I settled in to study was a great way to preserve not only my physical, but also my mental health. My time at the health club was non-negotiable, just like my study schedule. The physical outlet was imperative considering how much time was spent hunched over law books. Schedule in exercise time – even if it's just a brisk walk – find something you enjoy and do it daily, it will save your sanity.

I used a big calendar to set up the study schedule. I made sure the calendar was plenty big as this made it a more "in my face" presence, making procrastination difficult. Monday through Saturday I began studying at 9:30 am and finished studying for the day at 8:30 pm. I eased up on Sundays by taking the mornings off. Otherwise, Sundays mirrored the Monday-Saturday schedule.

Here is a sample study schedule for one day:

9:30 am-12:30 pm: 50 MBE questions / review answers

12:30 pm-1:30 pm: lunch

1:30 pm-4:30 pm: 2 essays / review model answers or complete a Performance Test

4:30 pm-5:00 pm: walk Mac (or just take a walk if you don't have a dog)

5:00 pm-6:00 pm: write out / review rule statements

6:00 pm-7:00 pm: dinner

7:00 pm-8:30 pm: 1 essay or write out rule statements or 33 MBE questions

A word about commitment to a study schedule. There really is no proverbial "magic bullet" in terms of how to commit to preparing for the bar exam. You really have to look deep inside yourself and decide if you are willing to spend several hours per day, day after day, week after week, preparing for a 3 day 18 hour exam (remember, beginning July 2017, it will be a 2 day exam). From my perspective there is no point in incurring the emotional and financial cost of those exam days, UNLESS you create an optimal opportunity to make the pass list. You create that optimal opportunity through a personal willingness to commit and adhere to a non-negotiable study schedule.

Once to my desk, I committed to 50 MBE questions UNDER TIMED CONDITIONS. You must practice under timed conditions so that when you take the bar exam you are comfortable working at the requisite pace. After completing 50 MBE questions in 90 minutes, I spent another 90 minutes reviewing my answer choices, making sure I understood the rationale for a correct answer, as well as (and just as important), the rationale for an incorrect answer. Again, it was relatively easy to eliminate two choices as incorrect, as they may have contained an incorrect rule of law or even a misstatement of the facts. The more difficult challenge was selecting the correct answer from the remaining two answer choices. Looking for key words from a rule of law often helped me select the correct answer choice.

Next, I would turn to essay material, with a goal to complete a minimum of two essays per day. I also spent time memorizing rule statements for each subject within a group; making sure I could write out short and succinct rule statements for each subject. For example, when working on Group 4 (Community Property, Wills, Trusts and Professional Responsibility) I'd write out rule statements for each subject. Then I'd write practice essays within that group of subjects. I'd then review the model answer, comparing my answer to the model answer. If I missed a particular issue, I'd study the model answer, paying close attention to how the issue was raised and discussed. Not only did I study how I missed an issue, I also tried to adapt or tailor my writing style to that of the model answer, paying particular attention to how an issue was raised and how the facts were used in the analysis.

I devoted Tuesday and Friday afternoons to Performance Tests, again, working under timed conditions. I chose to work on Performance Tests in the afternoon as this is when they are tested on the bar exam. Initially, I couldn't complete a Performance Test in the requisite three hours, but I gradually improved with practice. Once a Performance Test was completed, I would spend approximately 45 minutes comparing my answer to the model answer. It was very humbling in that my answer(s) often seemed disjointed and disorganized as compared to the model answer. I made a great effort to not only compare the **substance** of my answer to the model answer, but I also (just as with essay practice), compared the **language and writing style** of the model answer to my answer. I adjusted my writing style, struggling to have my answer read like a model answer.

I adhered to the above schedule until two weeks prior to the bar exam, at which point I stopped writing out full essays and Performance Tests and instead started outlining only. I would spend 15 minutes outlining essay fact patterns and 85-90 minutes outlining a Performance Test. Although I had already outlined and written out many of the essay fact patterns and Performance Tests, I repeated them, figuring the repetition couldn't hurt. Plus, given all of the studying I had been doing over the previous weeks, I really had no recollection of the essay fact patterns or details of the Performance Tests.

Having the above schedule written out (on my calendar) really kept my focus on commitment and studying – it minimized the human element of procrastination. If you are a self-disciplined person you can leave room for flexibility in a study schedule, but be brutally honest with yourself. If you are a procrastinator, or find yourself seeking out convenient distractions (checking email, texting etc.) forgo the flexibility, instead, draw up and commit to a schedule. If you take a formal bar review course you'll receive a schedule, you can use that schedule or adapt it to meet your needs. Either way, you MUST have and **commit** to a study schedule. Think of it as a roadmap that will help you navigate the bar exam subjects. Looking back I probably could have taken Sundays off, but I was serious (some would call me neurotic) about passing on my first attempt – I wanted to do everything possible to maximize my chances of making the pass list. I knew I did not want to walk into the bar exam **wishing** I had done more or regretting that I had not put forth a greater effort.

The final issue to address regarding the month of December, if you are taking the California Bar exam in February, is family, friends and of course, THE HOLIDAYS. If you are taking the July bar exam, the only holiday you will have to think about is the Fourth of July, not too distracting as far as studying goes, but for the February bar exam you will have Christmas and New Years to negotiate. Luckily these holidays are at the beginning of the bar review process and not in the middle or at the end. Although many people don't even begin studying until AFTER New Year's Day, I didn't want to wait that long, I felt there was simply too much to do. Instead, I began studying mid-December. This forced me to address bar review preparations along with the Holidays.

I realized my family and friends couldn't really understand (nor should I have expected them to) the amount of material I had to tackle. They didn't understand why I was worried about "a test" that was over two months away. I decided not to waste my time trying to explain it to them, instead I stuck to my plan and stayed focused on my goal of making the bar exam pass list in May. I took a break from studying on Christmas Eve,

Christmas Day and New Year's Eve. I felt I couldn't relinquish anymore time. I'm sure a few of my friends and family considered me obsessed, and they were correct, I was obsessed about NOT returning in July to do it all over again. I was on a mission – I wanted to pass on my first attempt.

3) Handwriting / Lap topping / Typing the Exam?

Although I had been typing all of my essays during law school, I choose to handwrite the bar exam. It was another decision (along with whether or not to take a formal bar review course) I agonized over. Because I had not handwritten an essay since the First Year Law Students Exam (FYLSE), my hand was not really "in shape" for handwriting almost anything, much less handwriting for 12 of the 18 hours of the bar exam.

Nonetheless, I chose to handwrite the bar exam, basing this decision on my concern that something could go wrong with a laptop (or typewriter) during the exam, leaving me stressed out and handwriting the exam anyway. Plus, I did not want to have anything more to think about other than making sure I knew the material and that I could do my best. I figured I would have less to worry about if I only had to concern myself with my favorite pens, pencils and earplugs, thus, I committed to handwriting the exam.

In making this decision as to whether to handwrite, typewrite, or use a laptop, the best advice I can give you is to do what will put you most at ease. I know of several people who used laptops, passed on their first attempt, and swore they could not have succeeded if they had handwritten the exam. One word of caution, once you select a certain method (either handwriting or typewriting) you cannot later change and choose to use a laptop after a certain date. I found this out the hard way. Half of the way through the bar review process, I decided I wanted to change from handwriting to using a laptop, but it was too late. I **was** permitted to change from **handwriting to typewriting**, but not **handwriting to using a laptop**. So think this decision through carefully before you decide NOT to use a laptop. Again, select the method that will raise YOUR comfort level – don't listen to what your classmates are doing, do what you know will work best for you. I knew that I didn't want to worry about any technological "glitches", so I opted for handwriting the exam.

4) Where to stay during the exam?

I had a few choices regarding where I would take the exam, which impacted where to stay during the exam. I had heard different ideas, for example, one of my classmates commuted three hours round trip every day of the exam as he wanted to be home with his family every night, thus, making the commute every day for three days in a row didn't bother him. I, on the other hand, would not have been able to sleep each night, worrying about a potential traffic jam, road closure or some other perceived catastrophic event – after all, they will not wait for you to arrive before starting the exam, even if you do have a good excuse. Also, even though my husband is the most supportive spouse anyone could hope for, I still didn't want the distraction of his presence during that three day period. Those three days were all about me, the material and the exam. I opted to stay on site at the hotel where the exam was being administered.

I arranged to check in Monday night prior to the exam, not wanting to move my car again until Thursday afternoon once the exam was over. If you can afford three nights in a hotel at or close to the testing sight, go for it! Staying right where the exam was administered really simplified things, in that all I had to do was waltz five minutes from my hotel room to the testing room. On the other hand, if you really hate big hotels, and being surrounded by all of the other bar examinees – in my case between 200-300 other examinees, you can (as some of my classmates did) stay off site at a smaller hotel or even a bed and breakfast.

It really comes down to knowing your comfort level. I needed to know I would be where I needed to be when each three hour session of the exam began. I did not want to be stuck in traffic or looking for a parking place. I opted for the path of what I perceived to be the least resistance, and booked a hotel room where the exam was being administered. All I had to do was walk across the hotel lobby. I figured I had enough to do just taking the bar exam; any details not conducive to maximizing my chances of making the pass list were eliminated.

A word of caution regarding staying at the test administration site. Try to minimize, or avoid altogether, talking with other examinees about the exam **during** lunch/dinner breaks. Each examinee will most likely see issues in a different way. If you waste, **and I do mean waste**, your time during lunch or dinner breaks discussing the exam, you are indulging in distracting, counterproductive and self-defeating behaviors that will not be helpful in passing the exam. Do not fragment your focus with discussion about the exam, instead, reserve all of your energy for making the pass list.

Remember, those three days are **your** three days. It doesn't matter what happened in the morning session when you know you are facing an afternoon session. Your only focus must be to do your best on each and every part of the exam. It doesn't matter if you think you didn't do well on a certain essay or Performance Test, or if you are sure you bombed the morning or afternoon session on the MBE. All that matters is that you give each and every part of the exam 100%.

It also doesn't matter how someone else did (or thinks they did) during a particular exam session. You will be tempted to discuss the exam with other examinees, but the cold reality is that it doesn't matter. Needless discussion will only serve as a distraction regarding the upcoming exam session. Remember, it is all about you, the material, and doing your absolute best during each three hour session of the exam. You cannot possibly do your best on an afternoon session if you are thinking about the morning session, or thinking about what someone **says** was an issue on an essay fact pattern. Thus, give all of your attention, focus and energy to each and every part of the exam.

However, if you must discuss the exam, wait until the exam is completed, then go to dinner and discuss everything you can remember. This is what I did with one of my classmates. He seemed to remember every detail about a Contracts essay fact pattern. After listening to him, I was sure I had failed the exam – I ended up with a horrible headache and certainly no appetite for dinner.

Chapter III - January

To repeat, some people don't even **begin** studying until the first week of January, I do not recommend waiting that long – not with so much to do, so much to think about, and so much material to cover. However, if you decide to wait until after the holidays, you absolutely MUST "put it in gear", and begin studying, in earnest, by January second, **at the latest**. Make a decision on a bar review course (if you're going to take one), set up a study schedule, and stake out a study space. Be sure all of this is done by January second so that you are ready to dive right in and get down to business.

An advantage I had by starting mid-December, was that by January first I had already done a substantive review of all bar exam subjects, along with organizing all of my outlines, plus, the six day MBE course was already completed. My desk was also set up, which had no other purpose other than bar review. NOTHING else happened at this desk. There was no computer, and thus no emails to check, nor were there any bills to pay or personal items to serve as a distraction. Basically, bar review owned this desk. Other than study materials, the only other item on this desk was my study schedule in the form of my study calendar.

It's worth repeating, having a study schedule forced me to stay on track and to stay focused, in that there was no room for negotiating bar review – it was **the** priority. Setting and meeting daily study goals created a genuine sense of accomplishment, in that I always felt a sense of satisfaction, ending a day of studying knowing that goals had been met according to schedule.

January dragged by. It felt as though I was in the depths of a dungeon. The days were cold and foggy, and were spent sitting at my desk with a blanket over my lap studying. I was totally dependent on my study schedule as it kept me moving forward through the 13 subjects. The bar exam still seemed in the distant future – in reality it was only seven weeks away. I adhered to my study schedule, memorizing rule statements, working MBE questions and writing out, **under timed conditions**, essays and Performance Tests. I pushed myself to stick to the requisite time limitation of no more than one minute and 48 seconds per MBE question, one hour per essay question, and three hours for a Performance Test. I spent two to three days on each group of subjects before moving on to a new group of subjects.

If I missed an issue on an essay, or selected the wrong answer when working MBE questions, I'd go back to an outline, or hornbook, and study that area of the law. I devoted equal time to understanding why I selected a correct answer, as I did to why an answer choice was incorrect. I kept a list of MBE questions where I had selected the incorrect answer and repeated those questions. I would often choose the correct answer the second time around, but not always. I used my incorrect answer choices as a way to identify areas of the law where I was weak or needed additional study.

By mid-January I was ready for a simulated MBE session. I chose not to do a simulated essay/Performance Test session as I felt *slightly* more confident regarding essay and Performance Test materials than I did about MBE questions.

I did as much as I could to simulate **actual MBE exam conditions**. For example, I prepared lunch ahead of time, unplugged the telephone, turned off my cell phone, and ate a good breakfast. I completed 100 questions in the "morning session" from 9:00 am until 12:00 pm. I took a one hour lunch break, although during the actual bar exam I had closer to 90 minutes. I completed another 100 questions in the "afternoon session" from 1:00 pm-4:00 pm. I took quick bathroom breaks when necessary and didn't allow myself to eat or drink anything during the "exam", unless I got up from my desk and had a quick drink of water. Remember, you are prohibited from bringing anything to eat or drink into the testing room on the bar exam

My goal was to get at least 150 correct answers (or 75%), as I figured if I did well on the essay and Performance Test portion then a 75% should be good enough to make the pass list. For my first simulation I scored a mediocre 138 correct answers out of a possible 200. My timing wasn't great in that I left three questions incomplete in the morning session and four incomplete in the afternoon session. There isn't a penalty for a wrong answer, so I guessed on those seven questions that I didn't have time to complete. Although 138 correct answers (69%) wasn't too bad, I knew I would have to improve if I was going to make the pass list.

Throughout the remainder of January, I continued working on essays and Performance Tests, writing out full one hour essays and full three hour Performance Tests. Time permitting, I also outlined essay fact patterns and Performance Tests, spending no more than 15 minutes per essay fact pattern and not more than 90 minutes for each Performance Test. To repeat, 15 minutes outlining an essay is the "rule of thumb" for a one hour essay. This leaves you 45 minutes to write the actual essay.

Your essay outline should be thorough, hitting the major issues and sub-issues spotted in the essay fact pattern, yet sufficiently brief, in that it shouldn't take more than 15 minutes to construct. With regard to a three hour Performance Test, spend no more than 85-90 minutes outlining your answer. For a 90 minute Performance Test, limit your time outlining to 45 minutes. The outline should provide guidance as you construct your answer, yet not so much detail that it becomes cumbersome and time consuming to create. Remember, an outline is a mere skeleton, which is fleshed out with your answer, whether it's an essay or a Performance Test.

I figured the more essays and Performance Tests I wrote, the more prepared I would be on "game day(s)". Not only do you want to be sure and write out and outline essays and Performance Tests, you must, without a doubt, outline and write out "crossover" questions. As previously stated, crossover questions are those essay fact patterns where two or more subjects are addressed. Remember, there are 13 subjects the bar examiners can test, plus Remedies, thus, the easiest way for the bar examiners to "slip" in an additional subject or two is with a crossover question. Criminal Law, Criminal Procedure and Evidence are fertile subjects for a crossover question, as well as Corporations (now Business Associations) Civil Procedure and Professional Responsibility.

Again, Professional Responsibility is testable with any subject. The State of California in general, and the Committee of Bar Examiners in particular, appropriately view Ethics and Professional Responsibility as topics of utmost importance. They want lawyers who are ethical and understand how to adhere to the rules of professional conduct. If you have an attorney in an essay fact pattern, be on the lookout for a violation of a rule or rules of professional conduct. If the attorney is not conducting himself ethically, discuss it thoroughly – show the grader, via a solid discussion, that you recognize the breach. Professional Responsibility is almost always tested in some capacity, so go in to the bar exam looking for a discussable issue regarding this topic.

Practice, Practice, Practice

I cannot overemphasize the importance of writing practice essays under timed conditions. Writing out **full practice** essays allows you to determine if you are able to formulate both sides of an argument in the allotted time. I know of only one person who didn't write out numerous practice essays and passed; I know of many more who didn't take the time to write out practice essays and failed. Furthermore, the process of writing out essays exposes you to the various ways issues can be presented in a given set of facts. I usually missed an issue NOT because I didn't understand the law or have a rule memorized, but rather, because I hadn't **considered** a particular issue could arise in a particular way. This is why writing numerous practice essays is so valuable – because it provides an opportunity to see issues presented in various ways.

Once you see an issue in a unique or novel way, you're less likely to miss that issue in the future. Plus, on the actual exam you must allow for some nerves and anxiety. If you've written out numerous essays, anxiety is minimized (although probably not eliminated), thus, with anxiety minimized all of your energy can be channeled towards the task at hand, i.e., identifying issues, providing the applicable rule of law, analyzing the issues, and drawing a well-reasoned conclusion. You cannot do this unless you have done extensive practice. You want to walk into the exam **KNOWING**, (not wishing) you are prepared, and the best way to prepare is through extensive practice.

The final area of the exam I systematically tackled was the Performance Test. Recall the Performance Test, which accounts for 26% of your grade, is a method of testing your ability to solve a complex legal problem. The Performance Test contains the file (25-30 pages) which provides information about the client. Included in the file is the "task memo", which details your specific assignment. The second part of the Performance Test is the library (50-100 pages) which contains relevant AND irrelevant cases, statutes, and legislative provisions. Fortunately, the law school I attended provided instruction on how to handle a Performance Test. As discussed earlier, you'll face a Performance Test on the first and third days of the exam during the afternoon sessions. In other words the Performance Tests will appear during the fourth, fifth and sixth, and sixteenth, seventeenth, and eighteenth hours of the exam – after lunch when many people will find their productivity and mental acuity at its lowest. Bear this in mind when you are having lunch on the first and third days of the exam – there will be a Performance Test waiting for you when you return to the testing room.

My lunch on those Performance Test days consisted of plenty of protein and not much sugar or caffeine. I knew I didn't want the sugar rush followed by the letdown, nor did I want the diuretic or nervousness effect from too much caffeine. I just wanted to be cool, calm and focused.

The best way to prepare for the Performance Test is to (again) write out as many practice Performance Tests as possible. I know it is extremely time consuming, but there is simply no way around it – you absolutely must, without a doubt, and this is non-negotiable, write out full practice Performance Tests. I designated Tuesday and Friday afternoons as "Performance Test days". Again, I chose the afternoons to practice Performance Tests, because that is when I'd have to face them on the bar exam. I wrote out full Performance Tests under timed conditions, twice per week, beginning mid-December and continuing through mid-February. Two weeks before the bar exam the study plan shifted – more on that later.

This was my customized study schedule. To recap, six days per week, Monday through Saturday, I exercised every morning, then I'd study from 9:30 am until 12:30 pm. I took a one hour lunch break, then resumed studying at 1:30 pm. Every 90 minutes I took a 15 minute break. Some say you should work continuously for three hours as is required on the actual bar exam, however, I chose to take a break every 90 minutes; I figured I deserved it given how hard I was working. Around 4:30 pm I took another break for 20-30 minutes and walked Mac, returning to my desk by

5:00 pm for another hour. Dinner was from 6:00 pm-7:00 pm. After dinner I put in another "session" from 7:00 pm-8:30 pm. I usually watched television from 8:30 pm until 10:00 pm, as I found this was a great way to unwind and relax. This was my schedule for the months of December and January. Before I knew it February first was upon me.

Chapter IV - February

Although I was glad to see the first of February had finally arrived in that the long grueling days of studying would soon be over, I also felt a sense of urgency, realizing that the bar exam was now only three weeks away. I felt like time was running out. There was still so much to do before I was "ready". I began to lengthen my days, staying up most nights until at least 10:00 pm – so much for unwinding in front of the television. I figured I'd have plenty of time for unwinding after the bar exam.

By the end of the first week of February, I decided to try my hand at another simulated MBE exam. I again duplicated actual exam conditions – working 100 questions in the "morning session" from 9:00 am-12:00 pm. I took a one hour lunch break and completed the second 100 questions in the "afternoon session" from 1:00 pm-4:00 pm. I again struggled to maintain the requisite one minute 48 second pace per question, guessing on five questions in the morning session and four questions in the afternoon session. My overall score of 149 correct answers offered encouragement, yet, my timing still seemed problematic. I knew I would have to watch the clock carefully on the MBE section of the bar exam in order to complete all 200 questions in six hours.

Ten days before the bar exam my study strategy changed. Instead of writing out full essays and Performance Tests, I switched to outlining. This not only saved time in the final days of studying, but it also exposed me to numerous additional essay fact patterns and Performance Tests. A word of caution however, **do not** switch to outlining essays and Performance Tests unless and until you are confident that you can write a passing essay in one hour, and a passing Performance Test in three hours, otherwise you should continue to write out full essays and Performance Tests under timed conditions.

As far as essays went, the more fact patterns I looked at, the more I was able to see how issues could arise in different ways – ways I hadn't previously considered. I read as many fact patterns as possible, hoping to miss issues now, during practice, rather than on the actual exam. I was encouraged when I saw an issue presented in a novel way, this meant I had a good chance of NOT missing it on the actual bar exam.

Along with issue spotting essay fact patterns, I drilled rule statements repeatedly, until I felt I knew them **at least** as well as my own name. Recall, rule statements are short and succinct phrases which provide the elements of a rule of law. You must have your rule statements memorized in order to thoroughly analyze a legal issue. I also integrated rule statements into my MBE practice. For example, if I was working on Evidence MBEs, I'd check the correct answer and then also write out the rule statement tested by the question. This not only reinforced rule statements, but it also gave me feedback as to how well I understood the law tested by the MBE question.

Performance Test practice also shifted. Instead of writing out two full Performance Tests per week, I wrote out one full Performance Test and outlined two (spending no more than 90 minutes outlining each Performance Test). Again, only if you are certain that you can write a passing Performance Test in three hours should you then move on to only outlining the material. The final step, after writing out and outlining Performance Tests, is assuring that you are familiar with all of the various tasks that can possibly be tested.

Often people who have worked in law offices or lawyers from out of state taking the bar exam struggle most with the Performance Test. All of their practical experience gets in their way, thus, instead of doing what the task memo directs them to do, they do what they would do in their own practice, or they do what they **think** would be preferable. This is a fatal error. The Committee of Bar Examiners expects you to follow the **exact** instructions as laid out in the task memo. Follow the instructions and you will be fine. Do something else, that you think is a more practical or better solution (and very well may be) and you will likely not receive a passing grade. Remember, it is very difficult to compensate for failing a Performance Test, because one Performance Test has the point value of two essays.

Remember, the task is the specific assignment that must be completed on the Performance Test. For example, a task may be drafting a letter to opposing counsel offering to settle a claim. Spend the necessary time and become **very familiar** with the various tasks as presented in the task memo. To do this, go back and review **every** Performance Test. Make sure you understand how to handle **any** task that may be presented. Remember, you do not want to be surprised on the exam, thus, now is the time, during bar preparation, to familiarize yourself with **all** of the various tasks as presented in the task memo.

There are many good resources on the market regarding the best way to prepare for the Performance Test. If you take a formal bar review course, you will receive a Performance Test book with numerous practice Performance Tests. You can also visit the CalBar website where you will find Performance Tests from previous bar exams along with selected passing answers. Take the time to become well acquainted with the Performance Test by writing out as many as possible. This will build your confidence that you will be able to write out a passing Performance Test in three hours.

Because the bar exam is a writing exam, one of my goals was to have either an essay or Performance Test selected by the Committee of Bar Examiners for publication on their website as an example of a passing answer. Setting that, perhaps unrealistic goal, motivated me to do my absolute best – both during bar preparation and on the bar exam – this goal was **not** accomplished. Neither an essay nor Performance Test of mine were selected for publication. But the main goal of seeing my name on the pass list **was** accomplished. I had to learn to live with not having one of my answers selected for publication, on balance, it hasn't been too difficult.

I maintained the above routine until the Sunday before the bar exam. Everyone has a different idea of what to do in terms of studying before, up to, and during the exam. I'd had enough. I designated the Sunday before the bar exam as my last full, genuine day of study. That Sunday consisted of drilling rule statements, outlining essays and reviewing the various tasks (from the task memo) that could be asked of me on the Performance Test. It didn't feel like a very productive day, but in retrospect it was extremely productive. I used that Sunday to mentally solidify the material – like a bowl of jello setting up. I was ready to get on with it. After two and one half months of studying eight to ten hours per day, six days per week, plus another five or six hours on Sundays, it was time to go and get it done.

Chapter V – Bar Exam Week

The Monday before the bar exam I packed my bags and prepared for the 90 minute drive to the hotel where I planned to camp out for three days and take the bar exam. I wanted to get checked into the hotel early so as to have enough time to scope out the test site. Each bar exam site is different, but, the location where I took the exam was a large hotel well equipped to handle the 200-300 bar examinees. I wanted to be sure that I was checked in and settled into my room early, so as to avoid the crowd.

I packed clothing for comfort, I didn't "dress for success" like some of the other examinees. One of my classmates wore a suit and tie to the exam. It looked impressive, but for me, getting dressed up in a business suit was out of the question, instead I opted for pure comfort: jeans, a short sleeve shirt and sneakers.

I packed a sweater, not knowing what the exam room temperature would be like. Turns out the room was warm and somewhat stuffy, I didn't need a sweater and was comfortable in only a short sleeve shirt. All of those bodies in the same room doing all of that concentrating must have raised the temperature. However, I talked with an examinee who took the exam at a different location, she said the testing room was freezing. So consider dressing in layers, and prepare for the room to be either hot and stuffy or cold and drafty.

The room where I took the bar exam did not have a wall clock, meaning I had to depend on myself to track my time. I think most testing sites are like this, the examinees are expected to have their own timing devices. Having a dependable, non-digital timekeeping device is crucial. Visit the CalBar website (or your states' bar website) to confirm, but when I took the bar exam, only silent analog timing devices of a specific size were permitted. If you prefer a small alarm clock rather than a wristwatch make sure it meets the specific size limitations. A visit to your states' bar web site will give you all of the detailed information you need. Remember, the bar exam – wherever you take it, is a strictly timed exam. Perhaps the tremendous time pressure is one of the things that makes the exam so challenging. Having a watch to track your time is an absolute necessity, managing that time is imperative.

Study Materials

I hauled all of my individual course outlines with me to the hotel. I didn't know how much time I'd have for studying, or even IF I'd want to study, but having all of my old familiar law school outlines with me created a sense of security.

While all of my outlines joined me for those three days, I made certain not to bring any essay, Performance Test, or MBE materials along. I had outlined and written close to 100 practice essays along with at least two dozen Performance Tests, plus I had done over 2000 practice MBE questions. At that point I decided it was best to just allow my brain to "marinate in the material".

Plus, I worried that if I tried to study I might outline an essay or Performance Test and miss an issue, shaking my confidence and sending me into a tailspin. The same was true for working MBE questions, I was concerned I might do a couple of questions and pick a wrong answer. I decided it best to leave well enough alone. I knew I had given it my all during the previous two and one half months, that I had done my very best to prepare – I had nothing left to give. My 10-12 hour days of immersion in the law were behind me now. I was done intensively studying.

Food

The hotel where I stayed offered room service, and had a couple of restaurants. You can eat at one of the restaurants if you choose, but a word of caution: the competition for restaurant space is fierce. Remember, the restaurants are for <u>all</u> of the hotel guests, including the 200-300 bar examinees. This means you could spend precious breakfast time (before a morning session) or lunch time (before an afternoon session) waiting for a meal, or worrying that you may not get seated in a timely fashion. You could find yourself wasting most of your lunch break standing in line waiting for a table. A good option is to order breakfast and lunch **the day prior** and have it delivered to your hotel room at a specified time. I could have taken this approach, but I was concerned a meal wouldn't arrive on time. If this happened I'd have to go into the exam either hungry, or rushed through a meal. I felt neither scenario maximized my chances of making the pass list.

In order to eliminate the possibility of these things happening, (which I perceived as major threats to my success) I instead brought along a cooler with fixings for my own breakfast and lunch. The contents were simple meal ingredients: cereal, fruit, nuts, yogurt, juice, canned tuna and smoked salmon. And of course, I had to have my coffee pot. As it turned out there was a small coffee pot in the room, so I ended up not needing mine.

My anxiety eased knowing I had breakfast and lunch covered – one less thing to think about. Dinner was different, I knew I would have time after a day of testing to either stand in line for a table, or wait for room service. I planned on eating dinner at the hotel restaurant, plus, I figured I deserved the treat of having a nice dinner after each day of testing.

Again, I just could not bear the thought of leaving anything to chance. I wanted to take away even a remote possibility of a "surprise". Looking back, I now realize I was trying to control as many variables as possible. I knew I had no influence over the actual exam material, so instead I tried to control the things I could. It eased my anxiety knowing I didn't have to depend on anyone for my meals during the exam.

Earplugs

Throughout law school and while studying for the bar exam I used earplugs, as I felt they improved my concentration and focus. So, of course, I brought a set of earplugs, and a back-up set, with me to the bar exam. If you've never worn them you really should give them a try. Although there is (of course) no talking during the bar exam, having earplugs filtered out the distraction of shuffling and turning pages, heavy sighing, and bodies shifting in seats. I really depended on my earplugs – as I said it improved my concentration and focus. Give them a try if you are looking to screen everything and everybody out.

Monday Night – Checking In

I checked into my hotel room about 6:30 pm on the Monday evening prior to the bar exam. I met up with a fellow classmate in the hotel lobby; we walked over to the testing room to "scope it out". We agreed to meet in the hotel lobby by the grand piano on Tuesday morning, so we could walk over to the testing room together. We timed how long it took to make the journey from the lobby to the testing room. It wasn't more than a few minutes, but we thought we'd better know in advance how long it would take – again, nothing was being left to chance.

We decided to take a preliminary look at the testing room. As it turned out, there were two large rooms for testing at the hotel; we were both assigned to the same room located downstairs from the main lobby. There were proctors from the Committee of Bar Examiners in place, they looked to be standing guard over the premises. We were allowed to peek into the room – actual entrance was prohibited. Looking back, we were behaving like little children, trying to catch a glimpse of Oz or Santa Claus.

We estimated there was space for approximately 150 examinees in our testing room. The room looked daunting with its several rows of long tables. We steadied ourselves for the upcoming three days, or 18 hours, or as I chose to frame it – it was merely six three hour sessions. After satisfying ourselves that we knew where we needed to be the following morning, and how long it would take to get there, we said goodnight and went back to our respective rooms.

I'm a big fan of organization, so upon returning to my room I unpacked my study materials, set up the coffee pot for the following morning, and laid out my clothes for "day 1". I'm not a fancy dresser, so laying out my clothes took all of five minutes. It was then I discovered I had forgotten my wristwatch. Panic set in! Beads of sweat formed on my forehead and upper lip. I tore apart my suitcase – no watch. I considered using my alarm clock, but it emitted a slight ticking sound. I knew this was one of the restrictions – the timekeeping device had to be silent. Instead of settling in for a relaxing evening on the eve of day 1, I went to the hotel lobby to ask the front desk staff where I could find the nearest department store. I desperately needed a watch – or two.

I was comforted by the fact that a shopping mall was close, only minutes from the hotel, but irritated with the crowds. Seems it was President's Day, and along with President's Day comes sales, and along with sales comes shoppers – lots of them; the stores were packed with bargain hunters taking full advantage of all of the markdowns.

After navigating the crowds, and finding a department store, I went straight to the jewelry department where I purchased two watches; I figured I'd better have a "back-up watch" just in case. I made it back to my hotel room in time to review a couple of law outlines. The exam began at 9:00 am the next morning, so it was "lights out" by 10:30 pm. I went straight to sleep, positive I was as ready as I could be for "Day 1".

Chapter VI – Tuesday – Day 1

Tuesday morning I met my classmate as scheduled at the grand piano in the hotel lobby. As we walked the few minutes to the testing room, all sorts of oddities jumped out at us. The most amazing sight was seeing people **actually studying** in the hallways outside the testing room. One woman had on a headset, listening to bar review CDs as she recited rule statements, another person was reviewing flash cards, while a third was reviewing law outlines. Others were pacing back and forth like caged lions waiting for their next meal. I kept my distance and tried to stay focused.

As I entered the testing room, I produced my admittance card (issued by the Committee of Bar Examiners) along with photo identification. The room consisted of long tables numbered in such a way as to correspond with the number on the admittance card. I found my seat and sat down, placing my admittance card along with my photo identification in front of me on the table; I folded my hands and waited for instructions.

Because I had taken the First Year Law Students Exam (FYLSE) twice, I was familiar with the testing format implemented by the Committee of Bar Examiners. The FYLSE, also referred to as the 'Baby Bar', is a 7 hour testing day that the California Committee of Bar Examiners requires students of non-California accredited law schools to take at the end of their first year of law school. Because the law school I attended was online, I was required to take this exam. It has a miserable pass rate of approximately 20%. If you pass, you're permitted to continue your law studies beyond the first year. If you do not pass you cannot proceed towards obtaining your Juris Doctorate Degree. I managed to eke out a passing score on my second attempt, allowing me the "privilege" of completing my law studies.

Once inside the testing room, I noted the low level of chatter as examinees filed into the room. Some put their heads down, some were biting their nails, and others simply looked straight ahead. One guy had his hands folded in prayer as he looked straight up at the ceiling. The tension was palpable. We had all prepared in some way or another, and some were still preparing out in the hallway.

I chatted quietly with the people on either side of me, mostly out of nervousness. The woman to my left was taking the exam for her second time. She attributed being unsuccessful on her first attempt to lack of preparation regarding the MBE section. This time, she was "sure" she had prepared thoroughly and "felt ready".

The man sitting to my right was taking it for his fifth time, he "thought", but he admitted it could have been his sixth time, he "wasn't sure". He swore he had "just missed" passing on his third attempt. I didn't ask what had happened on the subsequent attempts. Hearing how many times he had taken the bar exam unnerved me – that was it! I'd had enough socializing.

There were five or six proctors in the room. Once everyone was seated, the lead proctor began reading the rules and instructions for taking the exam. These same set of instructions were read prior to every three hour session, but the first day prior to the morning session was the most time consuming, taking approximately 20-25 minutes, because in addition to reading the rules and instructions, a set of fingerprints and a handwriting sample were also collected.

The handwriting sample consisted of a silly meaningless paragraph about taking a ridiculous trip to some far off place. The only purpose of the nonsense you are expected to write is that the paragraph contains every letter of the alphabet. I guess if there is any question regarding who actually wrote an exam, the Committee of Bar Examiners has the handwriting sample for comparison. Seems to me all they'd have to do if they had a question as to who wrote an exam, is to call you in for a second set of fingerprints, but perhaps that would be just too easy.

On to the instructions. They consisted of rules about taking the exam. Important rules, such as no notes, cell phones, digital timing devices and/or talking during the exam. I cannot imagine anyone thought it would be OK to bring in notes or talk during the exam, but the Committee of Bar Examiners wanted to be sure we all understood the rules, regulations and limitations.

We were also informed that the morning session was a three hour session, and that we would be given one hour, five minutes and 30 second warnings in the three hour session. We were also instructed that once time was called we were to "stop writing immediately". One of the more important rules was the one regarding the prohibition of digital timing devices. The woman sitting to my left (the one taking the exam for the second time) apparently didn't read the rules, as she brought in a digital watch, which the proctors promptly confiscated until after the conclusion of the morning session. As a courtesy they agreed to come around hourly and notify her of the time. This at least would inform her when to start the next essay. While this was kind of the proctors, I knew she'd have no idea how to limit her time outlining, nor would she know how much time she had remaining on any one essay. She simply could not pace herself. You would think, if she had already taken this exam, she would have at least remembered the rules regarding timing devices. She was fortunate the proctors were willing to help her track her time.

Once these housekeeping details were complete, the lead proctor instructed the other proctors to pass out the sealed exam booklets along with blank paper for outlining, and three "blue books", which is where each essay is written. If you are using a laptop, you'll still receive blue books even though you'll be submitting your essays electronically. Blue books are distributed in the event there is a problem with your laptop, in which case, you would then handwrite your essays.

Back to handwriting the exam. The blue books aren't blue, but rather, are color coded to correspond with a particular essay fact pattern. You MUST write your essay in the correct blue book which corresponds to a given essay fact pattern, so be mindful and deliberate when writing your essays to ensure that you are writing your essay in the correct blue book.

Once all of the testing materials had been distributed, (sealed exam booklets containing the essay fact patterns, color coded blue books, blank paper for outlining) the lead proctor again emphasized the restrictions regarding stopping once time was called and the prohibition of cell phones and/or digital timing devices. When she was satisfied that all requisite instructions had been read and re-read, she made the announcement: "*You may break the seal* [on the exam booklets] *and begin*".

Tuesday morning (identical to Thursday morning) consists of three essays for completion in three hours. I took great care, checking more than once to assure myself that I was writing each essay in the correct blue book. I also took the essay fact patterns in order, not going through and reading each one, looking for my strongest subject. I thought that would have been a distraction and a waste of time. Instead, I checked my watch, put in my earplugs, broke the seal on the exam booklet, and went right to work on the first essay.

Again, the rule of thumb is to spend no more than one hour on each essay. Fifteen minutes should be reserved for reading and outlining the essay fact pattern; the remaining 45 minutes should be spent writing the essay. You **must** complete each essay, which means you must limit yourself to one hour per essay. **Do not** make the mistake of spending more than one hour on any one essay, as this will leave you with too little time to complete a subsequent essay. Make sure to give each essay equal time and attention – limit yourself to one hour per essay.

The first essay was a Constitutional Law fact pattern. I breathed a slight sigh of relief when I saw it was "ConLaw"[1]. I felt I had a good understanding of the subject from law school and I had done several practice exams during bar review. I spent slightly more than 15 minutes outlining and another 43-44 minutes writing my essay. I felt like I was doing "OK" so far. I wanted to limit myself to one hour per essay, so getting the first one done in one hour gave me some confidence – I was staying "on time".

The second essay was a Contracts fact pattern. I always thought Contracts and Real Property were my strong subjects, so I felt, again, a sense of relief seeing the topic was Contracts. It was a complicated set of facts, one which included both common law and Uniform Commercial Code (UCC) issues[2]. I struggled to outline and write my essay in one hour. There were so many issues to

---

[1] Constitutional Law addresses the interpretation and application of the United States Constitution.

[2] Common law is judge made law. Article 2 of the Uniform Commercial Code governs the sale of goods.

discuss and arguments to be made. Given all of the essays I'd written in preparing for this moment, I still spent an extra five minutes on my essay, and could have easily spent another twenty minutes writing what I thought would have been a more complete answer. This left me with only 55 minutes for the third and final essay.

The last essay was concerning. It was a Corporations[3] fact pattern which was my second least favorite subject (Civil Procedure being my least favorite). I did the best I could, easily outlining and completing the essay in the time remaining, yet, I didn't feel confident. I kept wondering what major issue I had missed; the fact pattern just didn't seem difficult enough. I still wonder how I scored on that essay, yet, I'm glad I never found out, as only unsuccessful examinees learn their essay scores.

Time was called. I had completed 100% of every essay. Again, you must complete every essay to have a shot at passing. Even if you can't go into the detail you would like on an essay, make sure it is complete. This at least gives you a chance at passing. As I understand

---

[3] Now called Business Associations.

it, the graders want to read a completed essay, if you don't complete an essay the graders simply cannot give a passing score. Remember, everyone is under the same tremendous time pressure, so do your absolute best to complete each and every essay.

Once time was called the proctors began collecting the blue books, scratch paper and exam booklets. All of these materials were then placed in a sealed envelope which corresponded with each examinees' identification number from their admittance card. When all testing materials were collected, an announcement was made as to when the afternoon session would commence. We were then dismissed as a group – just like a bunch of first graders.

I went back to my room for lunch – tuna salad, yogurt, walnuts and orange juice. I wanted to eat some protein to keep from getting hungry during the afternoon session, but nothing too heavy that might cause drowsiness. As I walked back to my room, I couldn't help but notice the noisy hotel restaurant, crowded with examinees. I was grateful to be headed for the peace, quiet and privacy of my hotel room. Once in my room, I restocked my ice chest, ate lunch, and forgot about the previous three hours. My mind drifted, and I began thinking about the upcoming three hours and the Performance Test which I would be facing.

At the agreed upon time, I met my classmate at the grand piano in the hotel lobby for the walk over to the testing room. The afternoon session was similar in format to the morning session (and all other sessions for that matter) – I produced my picture identification and admittance card which allowed me to gain entrance into the testing room. Testing instructions were again read by the lead proctor, blank paper was passed out along with a "blue book" for writing the answer to the Performance Test. Once the lead proctor uttered the words, *"You may break the seal and begin"*, the clock was running.

I monitored my time carefully by placing my wristwatch right in front of me as I read the "task memo", the file and the library. I wrote the time the exam began (1:30 pm) at the top of the page of the task memo and also wrote "2:55 pm". This reminded me when 85 minutes had passed, and that it was time to take a mini-break and prepare to write my answer. At EXACTLY 85 minutes or 2:55 pm, I took that much needed mini-break, and went to the restroom. Although I didn't really need to use the restroom, I needed a mental break because my head was swimming with so much information from the file and library. I took two to three minutes to use the restroom, throwing water on my face while I was there. I returned to the testing room and began writing my answer.

The Performance Test was an assignment from a supervising attorney. My job was to draft a letter for signature by the plaintiffs' counsel, offering to settle a personal injury case. It included issues of comparative negligence, permissive use of an automobile and negligent entrustment.

I finished with a whole 30 seconds to spare! With that remaining 30 seconds I skimmed my answer and underlined key words. Overall, I thought I'd done an adequate job, as nothing seemed too confusing. As time was called I felt good – six hours down, only two days, or, 12 more hours of testing to go.

I went back to my room and wasn't sure exactly what to do with myself. After all those weeks of preparation and anticipation I had made it through the first day of the bar exam and had survived. I had completed all three essays and the Performance Test. I monitored my time carefully and felt as though I had "held my own". I thought about going for a run on the treadmill at the hotel exercise facility, but decided instead to save my strength for the next day. In retrospect, a run probably would have been one of the best things I could have done for myself.

I went to the hotel restaurant for dinner, even though I hated the thought of sitting in a restaurant and eating alone. I saw a woman I had met at the six day MBE course I'd taken back in December, I went over to say hello – she wasn't doing well. Apparently she had contracted a sinus infection two days prior and had a splitting headache and earache which had lasted all day. Her eyes were puffy – she looked and felt absolutely terrible. She didn't feel like she had done her best on our first day of the exam. I offered a few words of encouragement, wishing her well for the following day. I promptly changed my order to "to go" and went back to my room to eat dinner, grateful that I felt well physically.

After eating dinner in my room, I reviewed a couple of law outlines, said my prayers and turned off the lights, knowing the following day I'd have 200 MBE questions to face in six hours. I **knew** I needed a good night's sleep.

Chapter VII – Wednesday – Day 2 MBE Day

I woke up Wednesday morning full of optimism and confidence. As I sipped my morning coffee, I reviewed law outlines and rule statements for the MBE subjects. I allowed 45 minutes to shower and have breakfast. Tuesday was behind me, by the end of the day I'd only have three essays and one Performance Test left. Plus, in some ways I was looking forward to the MBE section of the exam, except I was still a bit concerned about time management and working at the 1 minute 48 second pace I'd have to maintain in order to complete 100 questions in each three hour session

Both times that I'd taken the First Year Law Students Exam (FYLSE). I struggled with my timing. The first time I scored 77 correct answers out of a possible 100 questions. The second time I scored 83 correct answers. But timing was my weakness; for whatever reason I just couldn't keep up the requisite one minute, 48 second pace per question. On my second attempt at the FYLSE, I was only able to complete 92 out of 100 questions, forcing me to guess on the remaining eight questions, yet I still managed to answer 83 questions correct. I hoped I had improved, that timing wouldn't be an issue for me today, especially since I'd taken the six day MBE review course and done over 2000 practice questions during the previous two and one half months.

A little before 8:00 am I headed for the grand piano in the hotel lobby to meet up with my classmate for the short walk to the testing room. Neither of us spoke of the previous day – all of our focus was on the upcoming three hours.

The routine for gaining entrance into the testing room was identical as the previous day. I dutifully produced my admittance card along with photo identification, I found my seat (the same seat for the entire exam) and waited for the lead proctor to read the same set of instruction and rules we'd all heard twice yesterday.

Even though time management regarding the MBE had been problematic during bar review, I thought the MBE day would be an easier day in that I wouldn't have to spend six hours handwriting. Plus, I told myself, the correct answer IS given to you on a multiple choice question, it's just a matter of identifying it. All I needed was a pencil, earplugs, an eraser, and of course my analog watch.

As I sat down in my seat I **again** began thinking about my timing struggles; that I'd **have to** work at the one minute, 48 second pace per question. This meant I'd have to complete 34 questions in the first hour, 33 questions in the second hour, thus, leaving 33 questions for the final hour. I knew I had trouble keeping up this pace during bar review, but I also felt I had a good understanding of the MBE subjects. I started to feel confident and ready to take on the first 100 questions – I began to have a "bring it on" attitude!

The non-descript beige exam booklets along with answer sheets were passed out as the lead proctor read the all-important rules and regulations, including detailed instructions on where to put our identification numbers, name, and other identifying information. Once these administrative details were complete, we were reminded that we'd be notified at the one hour, five minute, and 30 second marks.

We were then instructed to, *"Break the seal and begin".*

As soon as I heard those magic words ("break the seal and begin"), I started my watch, which was set for 9:00 am. Next, on the exam answer sheet at question 34, in **very light pencil**, I wrote "10:00 am", 33 questions later, at question 67, I wrote "11:00 am", and again, 33 questions later, at question 100, I wrote "noon". This was the method I used to inform myself if I was working at the pace necessary to complete the first 100 questions within the allotted three hours. If you choose to do this make sure to write the times in very light pencil, AND make sure to erase these notations **before** time is called. This is extremely important, as the exams are graded electronically, thus, there cannot be any stray marks on your answer sheet which could possibly be misread by the computer during the grading process.

Furthermore, if you have not erased these notations **before** time is called it will simply be too late, as the proctors are extremely serious about everyone dropping their writing implements once time is called. They will not allow you to go back and do something as benign as erasing marks on your answer sheet. So be sure this is done BEFORE time is called.

I then went right to work on the first 34 questions – telling myself I **had** to complete them in one hour (or by 10:00 am according to the notation on my answer sheet). As I began working, I was stunned and shocked at the level of difficulty of the questions, especially the Real Property and the Contracts questions which typically are the longest and most complex questions of all of the MBE subjects.

The other challenge (besides time management) on the MBE section was switching back and forth between the various subjects. For example, there would be a Torts question, followed by a Real Property question, followed by a Criminal Law question. This made it impossible to focus on any one particular subject. Although I had taken two simulated MBE exams where the subjects were all combined, this, "doing it for real" seemed much more difficult.

I struggled to keep up the requisite pace, pushing myself to limit the time spent on any one question to no more than one minute and 48 seconds. At times this was unrealistic, especially with the Real Property and Contracts questions where the **question** itself was two or three paragraphs long. In contrast, some of the Evidence and Criminal Law questions were much shorter, allowing me to "make up" some time.

As I arrived at question 34, I noted it was 10:05 am, yikes, I was already running five minutes, or two to three questions behind the requisite pace. I tried not to panic, but knew I had to either pick up the pace or start guessing on questions that seemed too difficult – maybe I needed to do both.

I didn't want to sacrifice the entire exam by getting bogged down on the longest and most difficult questions, thus losing an opportunity to answer the shorter, more straightforward questions. A word of caution: if you decide to skip a question pay **very close attention** to the **numbering** on your answer sheet to ensure that you do NOT enter an answer choice in the wrong place. I checked my answer sheet every ten questions to be sure I was transcribing the intended answer choice next to the correct number on my answer sheet.

Because all of the questions are of equal value, and there is no penalty for an incorrect answer, it makes perfect sense to answer all of the questions, and not leave any questions blank. I decided to place a very light mark on my answer sheet next to the long convoluted questions and leave those blank. I told myself I'd come back to those questions towards the end of the exam.

By the time I arrived at question 67 it was 11:10 am – I was now ten minutes, or almost six questions behind the pace, plus, I had left six more questions blank which I had intended to come back to "later"; this meant I had 50 minutes to complete 46 questions. Things had definitely gotten out of hand. My heart started racing while my head swam. I felt a flush over my entire body, as though I was getting a gigantic menopausal hot flash!

In the final 50 minutes I increased my pace, as I began worrying that I wasn't going to complete the exam. I knew I couldn't leave any questions blank, and if it came down to it I'd pick "C" (I don't know why "C") on any questions I didn't have time to complete.

The lead proctor announced, *"Five minutes remaining"*. At this point I was on question 96. I skimmed through the remaining four questions, selecting an answer choice as fast as I could. With two minutes remaining, I returned to the six questions which I'd marked earlier in the exam for completion "later". I spent a mere 10-15 seconds on each question, reading the answer choices first, trying to spot a rule of law which could give me a hint regarding the topic of the question, then I skimmed the question, usually picking "C", unless "C" seemed completely wrong. It's fair to say I was really guessing on those remaining questions, as my focus and concentration was minimal at that point.

Then came the announcement: *"One minute remaining"*. I kept working, skimming my answer sheet row by row, making sure I hadn't left any questions blank. My heart pounded as the final warning announcement came: *"30 seconds remaining"*. I had selected an answer for every one of the 100 questions, I continued to scrutinize my answer sheet, frantically erasing any extraneous marks.

I heard the words I knew were coming: *"Time! Stop writing immediately!"* The simultaneous dropping of 150 pencils pierced the silence. We waited in our seats while the exam booklets and answer sheets were collected. A shared sigh was heard throughout the room, no doubt it was one of relief. I felt depleted, completely wrung out.

Once all exam booklets and answer sheets were collected, instructions were given regarding the time the afternoon session would commence; we were then dismissed as a group. As I exited the testing room I couldn't help but overhear other examinees talking about the exam. Some were saying how easy it was, most were just shaking their heads. I went back to my hotel room, again, walking by the crowded hotel restaurant, grateful to be heading for a place of peace and quiet. I ate a light lunch, even though the previous three hours had literally ruined my appetite – I tried not to think about what had just happened.

A woman from housekeeping knocked on my door, attempting to gain entrance so as to tidy up my room. I thanked her, told her my room was fine, I didn't need housekeeping. She looked a little concerned, as I hadn't let her in to tidy up the day before either. I had law outlines strategically placed throughout the room, I didn't want her rearranging anything. She settled for giving me fresh towels, and of course, more coffee.

As I went to the ice machine to restock my cooler, I met up with another examinee. We couldn't NOT talk about the previous three hours we had both just endured. I asked how she was doing. She said this was her third time taking the bar exam; she didn't feel the morning session had "gone well" – she didn't think she would pass – again. I offered some words of reassurance and returned to my room. I had a few sips of coffee and kept my focus on the upcoming three hour session. I knew I had to keep giving every part of the exam 100%. I brushed my teeth, threw some water on my face and headed for the grand piano in the hotel lobby to meet up with my classmate. It was time to go take on the next 100 questions in three hours.

The afternoon session was essentially a repeat of the morning session. The questions seemed every bit as difficult. I again, marked my answer sheet in a similar fashion as I had in the morning session. To keep myself on target I aimed for 3:00 pm at question 34, 4:00 pm at question 67, and 5:00 pm at question 100. I again, struggled to keep up the requisite pace. At question 50 I took a quick one minute bathroom break and had a sip of water. The time seemed to be flying by at lightning speed. On average, I was running anywhere from three to four questions behind the requisite pace.

When the lead proctor announced, *"One hour remaining"*, I was on question 63. It was worse than I thought – I was a full four questions behind the pace, plus I had left seven questions for completion "at the end". This meant I had 44 questions to complete in the one remaining hour. I picked up the pace, skimming questions and selecting an answer as soon as one looked correct. There was simply no time to ponder and/or second guess myself.

The shortest questions are typically in the area of Criminal Law and Evidence. I spent the least amount of time on these questions, rushing through them as fast as I could without totally sacrificing accuracy. I also hurried through Constitutional Law and Torts questions, unless the fact patterns were long and convoluted, then I gave them a little more time.

As previously discussed, eliminating two incorrect answer choices was relatively easy, the more difficult aspect of the exam was selecting the correct answer from the two remaining choices. Often the difference between a correct or incorrect answer came down to one word. This, in my opinion, is what makes the MBE portion of the bar exam so challenging. You're not only under tremendous time pressure, but unless you read carefully, you will miss a key word that can make the difference between a correct and incorrect answer. I worked as carefully as I could to read every word before selecting an answer. Again, as I entered my answer selection on the answer sheet, I made sure I was entering my answer choice next to the **correct number** on the answer sheet.

The other tricky aspect of the exam is that there may be three or four questions concerning one fact pattern, but the questions are not arranged consecutively. For example, at question 15 there may be a long convoluted fact pattern followed by one question. You may then see the **same** long convoluted fact pattern 20 or 30 questions later with another question regarding this fact pattern. Then, another 15 or 20 questions later, there will be another question regarding **this same fact pattern**.

This required reading the same long complex set of facts three or four times. This was extremely time consuming; I actually found it to be rather bizarre if not somewhat sadistic, it was as Yogi Berra once said, it was "déjà vu all over again".

Finally, I heard the announcement: *"Five minutes remaining"*. I was only on question 96; I still had four more questions to complete, PLUS the seven questions I had left blank with plans to return to those questions "at the end" – now this WAS the end! I had only five minutes to complete 11 questions. Impossible!!!

My heart raced as I selected answers to the four remaining questions in a record three minutes. This left me two minutes to complete the seven questions I had left blank. I couldn't believe what a mess I had made, how far I had fallen off the pace! I skimmed each of the remaining questions and filled in an answer choice on my answer sheet. Where the question was simply too long to have any genuine chance at a complete reading, I guessed. As in the morning session, I was determined not to leave any questions unanswered.

I took great care to clean up my answer sheet, erasing any extraneous marks. By the time the lead proctor announced, *"One minute remaining"*, I had filled in an answer choice for every one of the 100 questions. I went back over the exam and tried to re-read a couple of questions where I had guessed, but I felt like a passenger in a car going 100 miles per hour, focusing was completely out of the question.

I heard the lead proctor announce, *"30 seconds remaining"*. "Good", I thought, "this will soon be over!" I spent the final 30 seconds re-scanning my answer sheet, making sure I had completed all 100 questions, making sure all extraneous marks had been erased. Finally, in an authoritative tone, I heard the lead proctor: *"Time! Stop writing immediately!"* I had already put down my pencil. As in the previous three sessions, our testing materials were collected and we were dismissed as a group.

I was relieved, yet exhausted. I hoped my time management would have gone better. I wasn't optimistic about passing the bar exam. I felt I had simply guessed on too many questions.

I returned to my room and called Al. I told him how poorly the day had gone, how I had struggled with my timing and of all of the questions where I had guessed. I told him I was seriously considering coming home. I don't know if I really wanted to come home and just give up, but I felt there was no way I could pass the exam given my struggles with the MBE section. I reasoned there was no point in going through another six hours of testing.

I put forth a great argument for coming home, cutting my losses; how I could save on another night of hotel costs (even though I knew it was too late to cancel my last night's stay without being charged). Al offered his typical in depth, thoughtful words of encouragement and support – the same words he routinely uttered throughout law school when I would have my usual anxiety attacks after finals: "You did fine". I told him I didn't do "fine", how I'd struggled with my timing and grasped at answers. I told him about how many questions where I had guessed and about the tremendous time pressure I'd felt throughout the exam. I explained how difficult the questions were compared to all of the practice questions I had done during bar review. Al kept dispensing his signature brand of support and encouragement as he dryly said, "You did fine".

I gave up. I couldn't convince him that this time was really different, that I didn't "do fine"; I only wanted to come home if I could get him to see I was right. I guess I wanted an endorsement regarding bailing out on the exam, but he wasn't budging, and so I was stuck. I hung up the phone, resigned to six more hours of testing.

Just as the previous night, I was unsure as to what to do with myself. I again thought of going for a run, but I felt so deflated that I quickly dismissed the idea. I considered getting room service, but the thought of eating in my hotel room seemed unappealing.

To my relief, my classmate that I met at the piano before every testing session called and invited me to dinner. We went to a local restaurant, away from the hotel, where we hoped to evade any other examinees. We agreed in advance that there would be no discussion regarding the bar exam, we had no problem complying with the agreement.

Dinner was pleasant, it was an escape from the hotel and exam environment – even if only for a couple of hours.

I returned to my room around 9:30 pm where I reviewed a couple of law outlines, and knew the best thing I could do was get a good night's sleep. I decided I'd wake up, complete "day three" and go home. Given my performance on the MBE section of the exam, I mentally, emotionally, spiritually, and psychologically prepared myself for the strong probability of NOT seeing my name on the pass list in May, yet, I decided I would still give the final day 100%. I was spent. I turned off the lights and fell into a deep sleep.

Chapter VIII – Thursday – Day 3

The clock radio jolted me awake at 5:45 am. As I sat in bed cradling my morning cup of java, I gazed at 11 law outlines spread out on the queen sized bed, trying to decide which ones to review. Because Contracts, Constitutional Law and Corporations had already been tested on the first day, I put those subjects aside, hoping they would not reappear. In retrospect, there was some risk with this strategy. Although the Committee of Bar Examiners usually doesn't test a subject more than once on an administration, they are, of course, free to do as they choose. At any rate, I took the risk, and put those three subjects aside. I knew I had time for a quick review of three, maybe four, outlines – but which ones?

The first outline I picked up was Trusts. I liked Trusts in law school, plus I'd had some practical experience dealing with my mother's Trust the previous year, so I budgeted about 30 minutes or less to get through my Trusts outline. I drilled rule statements, then made sure I understood the subtle differences between the ten different types of Trusts.

Next was Real Property. I always liked Real Property, but thought it should have been divided into two subjects just because of the sheer volume of material. While in law school I had a brilliant professor for Real Property, which is probably why I liked the subject so much. I spent more time reviewing my outline than I had originally intended, there was simply no way around it given the copious amount of complicated material to cover.

Because Real Property review had taken so long, I only had time for one more subject. As I stared at the nine remaining outlines, I had no clue as to which one to pick. I thought about closing my eyes and picking one, but rejected that idea, as this WAS the final day of the exam; certainly I could make a selection based on a more pragmatic and informed method.

I recalled my favorite professor in law school, (the same professor that taught Real Property) saying Professional Responsibility is almost always tested on the bar exam in "some capacity", whether as a full essay or in a crossover question. I imagined hearing his voice say that, "it almost always appears on the exam".

Even though I'd taken the Multistate Professional Responsibility Exam (MPRE) the year before and scored well on it, I still didn't feel like Professional Responsibility was one of my stronger subjects, it always seemed as though it was just a conglomeration of rules. As there hadn't been any Professional Responsibility issues on day one, (or at least none that I'd seen) I thought maybe it would show up today. I reasoned that if I was strong enough in the other subjects, (that I hadn't reviewed) and a Professional Responsibility issue came up, I'd be ready. I used my remaining time reviewing Professional Responsibility, leaving myself 30 minutes to shower and eat breakfast.

This was it. Day three. The final day. I got dressed, looked around at my outlines and notes scattered about the hotel suite, then gathered my pens, earplugs, picture identification and admittance card as I headed off for the piano in the hotel lobby to meet up with my classmate. I was ready to take on hours 13, 14 and 15 of testing.

The proctors greeted us as though we were old friends, their three days of testing was also coming to an end, albeit, far easier than mine. Examinees chatted, some about how they were going to celebrate when the exam was all over. I just tried to stay focused on the upcoming three hours.

Although I'd slept well I was edgy, the chatter in the testing room seemed particularly loud, and I felt generally fatigued. I knew there was only this final day and then it would be over; if I didn't pass this time I'd have to wait until July to repeat the exam, IF I repeated the exam. The problem with repeating the exam in July, is I would be required to get right back into the study grind as soon as results were released in late May. This was all too much for me – I felt tired just thinking about studying for the bar exam all over again.

Once we settled into our seats the lead proctor, again, began reading the same set of instructions she had read on days one and two. I was beginning to get annoyed, I wondered if she thought we were dumb or just had poor memories, or maybe both. I wondered why I had to listen to her say the same thing for the fifth time in three days. Intellectually, I understood, but emotionally, I was tired of listening to her repeat herself. I wanted to plug my ears just like a second grader, and block her out. Yes indeed, I was edgy.

All of the same materials were distributed, blank paper for essay outlining, sealed exam booklets, and the all-important color coded blue books. On cue from the lead proctor, I heard the all too familiar words, *"You may break the seal and begin"*.

I checked my watch and went straight to work on the first essay (labeled essay # 4). It was a crossover question containing issues of both Evidence[4] and Professional Responsibility[5]. At first I couldn't believe my luck in that it hadn't been more than an hour since I'd reviewed my Professional Responsibility outline. Before I began writing, I checked to be sure I was writing in the correct "blue book". Remember, you MUST write each essay in the correct corresponding blue book, so be very deliberate about checking which blue book you are writing in, of course, if you are using a laptop for the exam you won't have this to think about unless you have a problem with your laptop.

---

[4]That body of law governing the proof of facts.
[5] The expected legal, moral and ethical conduct of attorneys.

I spent 15 minutes outlining and another 50 minutes writing my essay. This was not good, I knew I should spend no more than one hour on each essay, but I wanted to write as complete an answer as possible. I knew I'd have to compensate for the lost time on the next essay.

I turned to the second essay labeled essay # 5. It was a Real Property[6] essay fact pattern concerning issues of joint tenancy with right of survivorship and landlord tenant issues. I again, felt so lucky in that I had just reviewed the subject of Real Property in my hotel room that morning. It was a complex fact pattern in that the analysis depended upon whether the parties were in a "lien theory" or a "title theory" jurisdiction. Of course the facts didn't specify the jurisdiction of the parties. I analyzed the facts from the perspective of **each** jurisdiction, naturally, the conclusion differed depending upon the jurisdiction. I spent 18 minutes outlining and another 50 minutes writing my essay. I felt I'd written an excellent essay, a real masterpiece, but I had left myself **only 47 minutes** to outline and write the final essay!

---

[6] Law governing various forms of property ownership.

Beads of moisture formed on my forehead. My palms were sticky and my heart felt like it was skipping a few beats. Why hadn't I stuck to the one hour per essay rule? I had written dozens of practice essays within one hour during bar review, yet, here I was on the bar exam spending too much time on one essay at the expense of another.

I turned to the final essay. I couldn't believe my eyes. TRUSTS!!![7] The three essays I had selected for review that morning were the **same three subjects** on this mornings' bar exam. What were the odds??? I thought I should run out and buy a lottery ticket as soon as the bar exam was over.

There was no time for a formal outline, I read the fact pattern and issue spotted along the way. I scribbled a few notes and began writing my essay. The question was a usual complicated Trust scenario, with three or four parties all claiming a superior interest to the Trust assets. I could have easily spent a full hour on that essay, instead I cranked out an answer based on the few scribbles I'd made in the margins of the fact pattern.

---

[7] Now called Wills and Succession.

By the time I heard, *"One minute remaining"*, I had completed the entire essay in a record 46 minutes! I spent the final one minute skimming what I had written – underlining key words and phrases. Finally I heard it: *"Time! Stop writing immediately"*, upon which I heard the collective dropping of pens.

I'd done it! Even though I had mismanaged my time, beginning with the first essay, I had completed all three essays within the allotted three hours. As all of the exam testing materials were collected, I thought: "This is definitely not the way to handle an essay writing session on the bar exam". I was the poster child for what NOT to do when it came to time management and essay writing. I knew not to spend more than one hour per essay, yet, the fact patterns seemed so complicated, as though they cried out for a complete and thorough analysis.

Once all testing materials had been collected, the lead proctor informed us when the final afternoon session would begin. We were once again, for the fifth time, dismissed as a group. As we all filed out of the testing room, there was some dull chatter, overall the mood was serious and somber, especially compared to what it had been three hours earlier.

I joined up with my classmate. We broke our own rule and began talking about the essay questions. He asked me what I thought of the Real Property question, I told him I thought it was difficult, especially since it required a "lien theory" AND a "title theory" analysis. He looked surprised and puzzled, asking what I meant. Rather than trying to explain the differences between the two theories, I said it probably wasn't important – probably a minor issue. I figured if he hadn't discussed both theories he probably had not written a passing essay, but I wasn't about to say as much.

I had lunch in my hotel room for the final time before my pre-arranged late check-out. It was a simple meal, I gobbled down some nuts, yogurt, and an apple. I then packed my clothes and gathered up my law outlines. I was ready to clear out of that room, I had been pretty much confined to it, and the testing room, for three days – I was ready to "breakout". It took two trips to get all of my possessions (mostly law outlines) loaded into my car. Room check-out went smoothly, I was grateful I didn't have to waste much of my lunch hour standing in line in the noisy hotel lobby. I had a full 45 minutes to spare before the final afternoon session began.

Hanging around other people waiting for the exam to start was a new experience. The prior two days, I had remained sequestered in the solitude and privacy of my hotel room, right up until the final minutes before each session began. Today, I had nowhere to go, so I loitered in the hotel lobby, watching all of the activity as guests checked in and out. The decibel level was high. I decided my hotel room wasn't so bad after all, I wanted to slink back to it, and wait there for the exam to begin.

I thought I would have a cup of coffee (half regular and half decaffeinated), but was worried about the diuretic effect of coffee during the final three hours of the exam, so I decided I'd have just a few sips, just enough to get a "little jolt", but not so much that it would cause me to run to the bathroom every ten minutes.

As I stood around the hotel lobby, carefully monitoring and savoring each sip of precious java, I began chatting with a woman, another examinee, who seemed quite nervous, as she fidgeted with her hair and nails. She said she had been taking "it" since 1997, although she thought she had missed one or two administrations. According to my calculations, if the bar exam is offered two times per year, and she had been taking "it" since 1997, then she had taken the bar exam approximately 15 times. I was stunned and speechless – and being speechless is a rarity for me. I asked how she felt she had done over the past two days, she flashed a weak smile, saying she didn't think she had "done very well". She went on to say she was considering going into nursing if she didn't pass this time. I didn't tell her I was a nurse and had been for 25 years. I nodded in casual agreement, saying I'd heard it was a good profession. I excused myself, thinking, "What is going on? Taking the bar exam since 1997?" I knew I couldn't keep taking this exam, I hoped this would be my first and last attempt.

By now, it was getting close to time for meeting my classmate, so I wandered over to the piano in the hotel lobby. We walked over to the testing room, pretty much in silence, neither of us wanting to discuss the exam. As we approached the testing room, we noticed people **still studying** for the exam, some sitting on the floor, backs against the wall, others just standing around. I couldn't fathom studying at that point, I just wanted to get in the testing room and get it done. We stood in line and waited for the doors to open. When they finally did, we all knew the drill. We obediently produced our picture identifications and admittance cards. The proctors greeted us, almost casually, as they congratulated us for making it to the final three hours of the bar exam.

I found my seat, just like I had done five previous times over the past three days; I sat down, and waited for the lead proctor to begin her final recitation of the all-important rules and regulations. As I looked around I noticed several empty seats, some examinees had bailed out, not making it for the sixteenth, seventeenth and eighteenth hours of testing.

Once the lead proctor began speaking, I completely tuned out, refusing to listen to her repeat herself for the sixth time. I had almost memorized the exam instructions, I just wanted to get the exam started. Once all testing materials were distributed, on cue, the all too familiar words were spoken, *"You may break the seal and begin"*.

As on Tuesday afternoon with the previous Performance Test, I began by reading the "task memo". This time the task was to draft an appellant's brief (statement of facts and argument only). The appeal was from a trial courts' finding that a marital settlement agreement was invalid based on the drafting attorneys' failure to make an adequate conflict of interest disclosure. This wasn't as straightforward as the previous Performance Test. I read the "file" and "library", making notes as I went through the numerous pages of material. I monitored my time carefully, **promising** myself that no matter where I was in terms of reading through the material, I would leave a full 90 minutes to write my answer.

After 85 minutes, I still didn't know what to write, my outline wasn't even an outline, but rather a disorganized set of notes. I needed a break. I went to the bathroom, threw some water on my face and kept thinking that I needed to "get with it"!!! I looked in the mirror and noticed how weary and beaten down I'd looked, such dark circles under my eyes, I needed my makeup bag – at least a little lipstick. It could have been the poor lighting, but, no, I looked completely worn out.

I returned to my seat and began writing my answer, which seemed disjointed and disorganized. Because I handwrote the exam, I didn't have the luxury of rearranging whole paragraphs, like I could have done if I had used a laptop. At one point, I accidently left out an entire section of text. I crossed out what I hadn't meant to write, wrote what I had forgotten, and kept right on going to the next paragraph.

With about 45 minutes remaining, I heard, through my earplugs, the soft drone of either a lawnmower or leaf blower in the distance. As I looked toward the window, in the direction I imagined the noise coming from, I noticed a weak faint ray of February sunshine streaming through the window. At that moment, I swore I'd never again put myself through another 18 hours of testing. If I didn't pass this time I wasn't coming back to try again.

The announcement came, *"Five minutes remaining"*. My answer was nearly complete; I only had another three or four minutes of writing left. I kept frantically writing, doing my best to be organized and "sound lawyerly"- whatever that meant. I desperately penned my answer, my eyes glancing every few seconds between my paper and the sweep hand of my analog wristwatch. By the time I heard *"30 seconds remaining"*, I was already done – I had no use for the final 30 seconds. I kept my pen in hand only because I could, it was only 30 seconds, but it was MY 30 seconds.

The final proclamation was made, *"Time! Stop writing immediately!"* The sound of the simultaneous dropping of all of those examinees pens is one I will always remember, it marked the completion and accomplishment of three days/18 hours of testing. I had generally been preparing for that moment for over four years, and intensely preparing for the past two and one half months. As all the pens dropped, the nervous chatter began.

The bar exam was done! I asked the man to my right (the one taking it for either his fifth or sixth time) how he thought he had done, he shook his head, saying he hadn't finished the Performance Test, he thought he "was sure" he hadn't passed. Although I figured he was probably right if he hadn't finished, I reassured him he really couldn't know until results were released. I didn't speak with the woman to my left who was taking the exam for her second time, although I couldn't help but notice her doing a lot of head shaking.

Once all exam materials were collected, we were, for the sixth, and final time, dismissed as a group. A weak applause arose from some of the more enthusiastic examinees. I just wanted to go home to Al, and the champagne I had asked him to be sure and have chilled.

As I made the 90 minute drive home, I kept thinking about how I had selected the **exact** three subjects for review that had been tested on that final day. It seems I was moved to select those subjects for review. I kept thinking that selecting **those three** subjects was against all of the odds. I wondered how it happened. I concluded I had received help from the heavens and the universe that morning as I gazed at those 11 law outlines – and picked the **precise three subjects** that were tested. Its help I'm sure I needed, and I will always be grateful for having received it.

When I got home, Al and I had a much deserved toast. This bar exam experience was as much his as it was mine. He had endured four plus years of law school and numerous missed dinners and evenings together, not to mention all of my broken promises that I would study "only until 8:30 pm tonight". I was exhausted, relieved, depleted and all at the same time overwhelmingly satisfied knowing that the bar exam was completed. I savored each sip of champagne and was so grateful to have it all done.

Chapter IX March, April, May – The Wait and the Results

Al and I loaded up the car Friday morning for the seven hour drive to Los Angeles – I was graduating, with honors the following Saturday morning. After all of those years of study and preparation, culminating with the bar exam, graduation was the proverbial "icing on the cake". For nursing school graduation I received a pin, this was different, I wore a cap and gown and was "hooded". It was ceremonious and I loved every minute of it, including the luncheon reception, complete with a champagne toast following the graduation ceremony. During dessert, one of my classmates, who had passed the previous bar exam administration was sworn in. As he took the attorney's oath, I looked on in awe, wondering if I would ever be in his shoes.

That evening, after getting lost in Los Angeles traffic, Al and I drove to Malibu to meet up with a couple of my classmates for dinner. Our table looked out onto the Pacific Ocean. I had a martini and gazed out at the ocean waves, feeling a sense of contentment and accomplishment for having graduated with my Juris Doctorate degree, but I was especially relieved to have completed the California Bar Exam.

One of my classmates that met us for dinner didn't take the bar exam, he was going to wait for the July administration, the other classmate had taken the exam. As we waited for dinner to arrive, the classmate that had taken the exam began discussing the second essay fact pattern (Contracts). To my amazement he seemed to recall every detail as though he had a copy of the essay fact pattern in his back pocket. His interpretation and answer sounded far superior to mine. He droned on and on, discussing his answer with incredible detail. When I tried to present my interpretation of the question, he summarily dismissed my analysis, explaining how my perspective could not have possibly been correct. I felt myself shrinking in my seat. I began doubting myself, thinking maybe I **had** written a failing essay. When dinner finally arrived, I'd lost my appetite and had a pounding headache. The check came, we paid the bill and left, miraculously finding our way back to the hotel without getting lost. Sunday morning we loaded up the car and made the seven hour drive back to the Bay Area.

Monday morning at 8:00 am, I found myself in the radiology department of our local hospital having a stereotactic biopsy of the left breast, where fourteen separate specimens were collected. Within two days I received the results: Inconclusive. I was required to have a second, more extensive biopsy (a needle localization excisional biopsy). The earliest surgery date available was three weeks away – and so I waited – for another biopsy, along with bar exam results.

I was consumed by thoughts of the upcoming breast biopsy during the month of March, only occasionally thinking about the bar exam pass list. I finally had the second biopsy, receiving results two days later: Atypical cells, but no cancer cells. Relief washed over me as I had been holding my breath for almost a month. I saw my surgeon who recommended a repeat mammogram in six months. By then, I thought, I'd know if I made the pass list.

The recuperation period from the second biopsy took longer than I had anticipated. By mid-April, Al and I made plans to get away to our cabin in the mountains of northeastern California for some cross country skiing. Although I tried to enjoy myself, I couldn't help but notice my decreased stamina. Between the bar exam, graduation, and two breast biopsies in as many months, I was exhausted. And then of course, there was the same endless question: "So how did you do on the bar exam"? I gave my stock rehearsed answer: "It was tough, it could go either way". As for the exhaustion, the only solution was time and rest.

By the time the first week of May arrived I had *almost* forgotten about the bar exam, it seemed so long ago that I had sweated my way through those three days. In fact, if it hadn't had been for all of those annoying people who kept asking the same question every time I saw them, I probably would have forgotten about the whole ordeal. But they kept asking: "Did you pass?" And I kept responding, "I won't know until the end of May". Then I'd see them again, maybe a few days later, and they'd ask, "Did you pass?", and I'd give the same answer, "I won't know until the end of May". This "dance" was frequently repeated, such that I couldn't help but wonder if anyone ever really listened when I responded.

The second week of May, Al and I took a three week road trip to British Columbia. Bar exam results would be released while we were away. The Committee of Bar Examiners, in what might be considered an act of mercy, releases the exam pass list **first** to the examinees at 6:00 pm PST on a Friday evening (when I took the exam it was the third week in May), then, 48 hours later, the exam pass list is released to the general public. Provided I had my identification number, issued by the Committee of Bar Examiners, I would be able to logon to the CalBar website and check the pass list for my name.

At 6:00 pm PST on the Friday the pass list was released, I was sitting around after dinner with some friends in British Columbia. Although I knew results had been released, I couldn't or wouldn't logon and check the pass list for my name. I realize now, I thought my chances of NOT passing were very real. If my name wasn't on the pass list I wanted to be home, with (as a friend from law school joked) "all sharp objects removed from the house". As I sat there, not checking the pass list, I pretended not to care, but what I was really doing was holding out hope that I **had** passed for as long as possible. I refused to logon and find out if my name was or was not on the list. Al never pressured me – he just let it go.

As we drove back from British Columbia, results had already been released for four days to the examinees and two days to the general public. Crossing the California border, I decided to check my cell phone for messages, thinking if I **had** passed surely someone would have called and left me a congratulatory message. Once into my voice mailbox, I heard the abrupt female generated computer voice, *"You have no messages in your mailbox"*. "Darn!" I threw down my cell phone as I made the big declaration to Al, "If I didn't pass I'm not taking it again". Al offered his usual calm and considered words of comfort and support, "You passed". I just gazed out the window as we headed south on Interstate 5.

We arrived home at 6:00 pm on the Wednesday evening following the release of the pass list. Results had been available for five days to examinees and three days to the general public. After unloading the car, I decided I could no longer put off not knowing. But, instead of logging on to the CalBar website and checking the pass list, I decided I'd first check my email. There it was, a note of congratulations from one of my classmates, and then another, and another! Altogether I had 12-15 emails from classmates and friends congratulating me on passing the bar exam. At that point, I figured it was safe to check the CalBar website pass list to confirm what seemed to be a reality. I logged on and found my name – there were actually **three** "**Navarros**". I checked carefully, reading my own name over and over to make sure it really **was** MY NAME. I cried, laughed and shouted all at the same time!!! My daughter and Al were on either side of me, "pretty good", my daughter said, and Al, well Al rendered his typical words of wisdom, "I told you you'd pass".

Chapter X – Getting Sworn In

I could have easily been sworn in at the beginning of June at a "mass swearing in ceremony" at a large auditorium in Oakland, California. Instead, I chose to wait and take the attorney's oath as part of my law school's July graduation ceremony. Al and I flew down to Los Angeles, this time there was no driving seven hours and arriving exhausted. We checked into our hotel room, then went to the hotel restaurant for a lovely dinner; what a contrast this trip was as compared to our trip five months prior. Passing the bar exam was such an incredible feeling of accomplishment – I was there to get sworn in, **and**, I didn't have a breast biopsy waiting for me when I returned home. I was able to just enjoy the entire experience.

I woke up Saturday morning and went to the hotel exercise facility for a run on the treadmill. A sense of satisfaction and achievement overwhelmed me, I couldn't believe I had done it. After the graduation ceremony, I took the attorney's oath along with another one of my classmates – we were sworn in as "attorneys at law" and "officers of the court", it's a moment I'll always remember. All of those hours of bar exam preparation, consisting of numerous practice essays and Performance Tests, and literally hundreds of MBE questions had finally paid off. I'd accomplished what I had set out to do four plus years earlier. I'd passed one of the most difficult bar exams in the country, and had done so on my first attempt. Moreover, I had beat incredible odds by passing without taking a formal bar review course. But best of all, I didn't have breast cancer.

Final Suggestions / Parting Thoughts

Here are some final suggestions which I believe are applicable not only to the California Bar Exam, but to any states' bar exam, or any other rigorous exam you are facing.

1) **Set up a study space** – this space should be used exclusively for studying. No miscellaneous "things" should be on this desk which will only serve as distractions. If you are using a laptop for the exam, disable your internet connection so you are not tempted to check emails or search the web when you **know** you should be studying.

2) <u>**Commit to a study schedule**</u> – whether you take a formal bar review course, or go it on your own, you will need a solid study schedule to direct your efforts **every day**. Having a schedule gives you direction and focus on a **daily basis**. You must have a schedule in order to succeed. You cannot approach every day studying what you feel like studying, or making it up as you go

along. Consider your study schedule to be a roadmap; you wouldn't take a trip without looking at a map, same goes for preparing for the bar exam, or any big exam. You MUST have a study schedule.

3) **Schedule in free time** – scheduling in free time, or "down time", is as important as study time. This includes time to go to dinner, watch a movie or doing whatever by yourself, or with your significant other. No one can, or should, study for any exam every waking hour. You need to be 100% present and available to do your best. This means 100% mentally, spiritually, psychologically, and physically present. In order to do this, you must take good care of yourself. You deserve and need to have free time, so schedule it in.

4) **Perceive the California Bar Exam as only six separate three hour sessions** – DO NOT look at the California Bar Exam as an 18 hour exam over three days. Reframe "it" as merely six individual three hour exam sessions. Take each session as a separate exam, it's much more manageable to think of it as such.

5) **Give 100% to each three hour session** – no matter how poorly you think you may have done on any one session, promise yourself that you will give each and every part of the exam 100%!!! (Remember how poorly I was sure I had done on the MBE section). It's not up to you to decide how you did, that's what they have bar exam graders for; all you can do is give each and every session 100%, then wait for results. (It's difficult, but everyone has to wait the same amount of time).

6) **Eliminate the nonsense from your life as you prepare for the exam** – this may be a difficult one, but do your absolute best to eliminate all people and activities that are essentially "time wasters". You can always reconnect with these people/activities after the exam, but during bar exam preparations time is precious; there is only time for studying and taking care of yourself as described in #3 above.

7) **Allow all non-emergent phone calls to go to voice mail** – unless a phone call is of a *truly emergent nature*, let it go to

voice mail. During bar review I only answered the phone for my husband and daughter; they both knew my study schedule and thus, knew not to call unless it was truly an emergency. All other calls went to voice mail and were returned at a scheduled time.

8) **Meet you daily study goals** – your study goals will come from your study schedule. Do your best to stay on track and meet your daily study goals. By complying with #7 above, meeting daily study goals is greatly facilitated.

9) **Stay positive before, during and after the exam** – I really struggled with this one, especially staying positive during the exam, but staying optimistic and positive is absolutely in your best interest. DO NOT listen to anyone tell you how hard / impossible the exam is – you **CAN** pass this exam. Yes, indeed it is challenging, but **YOU CAN DO IT!!!** Stay positive and visualize your name on the pass list – at all times.

10) **Know / Believe you can and will pass** – Believing you can pass is very similar

to #9 above, but **you must** believe you can and will pass. With every bar exam administration there is a given percentage of examinees that pass…if some are going to pass, why not you??? Believe you will be amongst those that make the pass list.

Passing the California Bar Exam was, without a doubt, the greatest academic accomplishment of my life. It took all of the focus, discipline and determination I could muster. I like to think I was well prepared for the exam, that I thoroughly understood the material. I know I practiced extensively, however, as you can see, I still had difficulty managing my time and emotions throughout the process. I struggled and stumbled through various parts of the exam. Perhaps it's impossible to be totally calm and in control during those three days given the amount of material tested combined with the tremendous time pressure an examinee is placed under. But you have to keep telling yourself that you are as prepared as possible, and **you will give each and every part of the exam 100% right up until time is called in the final hour 18th hour**.

The bar exam is a terrific challenge, achieving a dream is overwhelmingly satisfying, I took an unconventional approach by not taking a bar review course and passed – if I did it, I **KNOW** you can too.

Epilogue

In April of 2006 our beloved border collie-husky mix Mac died at the ripe old age of 16. Al and I both cried as we brought him home from the animal hospital and buried him in our backyard. We planted a lovely purple hibiscus shrub on the site to mark the spot. He was a faithful companion to me as I spent hours and hours studying, not only for the bar exam, but also throughout my four plus years of law school. It took us three years to get another canine companion. We now have "Murry", a beautiful German shepherd / Golden Retriever mix, adopted from our local animal shelter.

My classmate, who I faithfully met at the piano in the hotel lobby (the one who hadn't seen the Real Property essay fact pattern "lien theory/title theory issue"), did not make the pass list. He never repeated the bar exam.

The classmate who I met in Malibu for dinner, the one who remembered all the details of the Contracts essay fact pattern, **did** make the pass list, sadly and suddenly, he died two years later of a massive cardiac arrest. My other classmate who joined us for dinner that night, (the one who was going to wait for the July administration) ended up taking the bar exam several years later, and made the pass list.

After the bar exam, I began working for an Elder Abuse attorney as an independent contractor, reviewing and summarizing medical records, assisting with deposition preparation, and preparing responsive briefs. In 2006, after we lost Mac, Al and I moved to our cabin in northeastern California for two years. We returned to the Bay Area in 2008, right as the recession hit, consequently, I went back to work as a nurse for a few years, but have since retired from the profession. I recently became certified as a personal trainer/yoga instructor, and work part-time at a local health club. I continue to work as an attorney on an independent contractor basis, consulting on medical-legal cases. I've also developed an interest in Estate planning, and am working towards expanding my practice in to that area. Gratefully and thankfully I have continued to enjoy good health, along with the love and support of my spouse and best friend, Al.

www.ingramcontent.com/pod-product-compliance
Lightning Source LLC
Chambersburg PA
CBHW030806180526
45163CB00003B/1157